Original Title: Cherished Connections

Copyright © 2024 Book Fairy Publishing
All rights reserved.

Editors: Theodor Taimla
Autor: Regiina Rannaveer
ISBN 978-9916-748-00-8

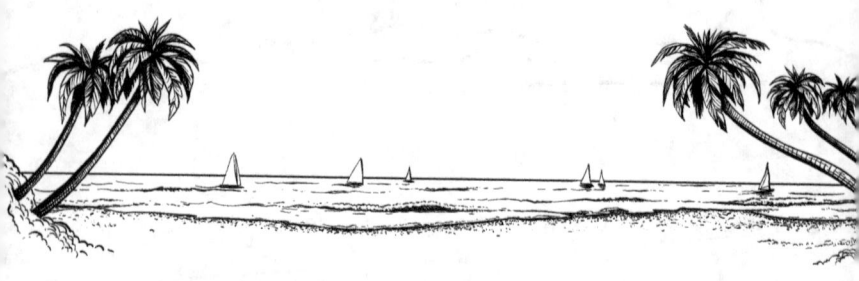

Cherished Connections

Regiina Rannaveer

Illuminated Manuscripts of Us

In the margins, our lives unfold,
Flecked with gilt, in colors bold.
Each letter, a story that we've composed,
Bound in leather, our chronicle enclosed.

Beneath the vellum, our secrets sleep,
Ink and pigment, layered deep.
Stories of love, of joy, and sorrow,
Penned today, but read tomorrow.

On pages bright, our dreams take flight,
Illuminated in the candlelight.
A tapestry of us, in hues so fine,
Our lives intertwined, by your hand and mine.

With careful hands, we trace our lore,
Each chapter better than the one before.
In this manuscript, so finely spun,
The tale of us, forever young.

Through years and miles, these pages will travel,
As time's mysteries slowly unravel.
A legacy of love that cannot rust,
Bound in the illuminated manuscripts of us.

Portraits Painted in Shared Hues

In the gallery of our creation, we stand,
Two figures cast in light's soft band.
Brush strokes bold, yet tenderly planned,
Our colors blend where our hearts land.

In every hue, a whisper of your spirit,
In every shade, the depth of our merit.
Together we're a spectrum, vivid and true,
In portraits painted in shared hues.

With every line, our stories intertwine,
In the art of us, your soul meets mine.
A masterpiece of love, deeply imbued,
In each other's gaze, endlessly renewed.

Time may age the canvas, but not our view,
For in our hearts, the paint remains new.
In the gallery of life, through and through,
Our portraits stand, in shared hues.

Whispers Woven into the Wind

With words unspoken, we converse,
Through the gentle breeze, our thoughts disperse.
Feelings float, in the air, softly encased,
In whispers woven, intimately traced.

Secrets told to the listening leaves,
Carried afar, beyond the eaves.
Each gust a carrier of silent sighs,
A symphony heard beneath open skies.

In the hush of dusk, when day is ended,
Our whispered words, in darkness, blended.
The wind, a conduit of unseen bind,
Carrying the tales of hearts entwined.

Though words may fade, as whispers do,
The wind remembers, keeps them true.
In every breeze, you'll find a trace,
Of our whispers, woven into space.

An Ode to Unspoken Bonds

Not all ties are seen, but felt within,
A silent pact, skin to skin.
In glances shared, no words need rise,
An ode to bonds, beyond the skies.

Through times of joy, and shadows deep,
These unspoken vows, we silently keep.
A comfort found, in the silent space,
A knowing look, a gentle grace.

In every heartbeat, in every sigh,
The unvoiced promises, that never die.
A tether, unseen, holding us tight,
In the absence of sound, our spirits unite.

No words can capture, the depth so profound,
In silence, our deepest connections are found.
An ode to the bonds, silently spoken,
Invisible, yet forever unbroken.

The Infinity of Intimacy

In the quiet space, where hearts dare to tread,
Lies the infinity of intimacy, unsaid.
A touch, a glance, a breath shared in close,
In these moments, the depth of our bond shows.

Beyond words, our souls speak clear,
In the language of love, we draw near.
A connection so deep, it transcends time,
The endless dance of yours and mine.

In the whispers of night, in daylight's embrace,
Our spirits mingle, in the silent space.
An infinity found, in the span of a look,
The unwritten chapters, of an open book.

Each gesture, each silence, a testament true,
To the boundless intimacy shared by two.
In the infinity of us, love finds its way,
In the unsaid, where our truest selves lay.

Entangled in Eternity

In the weave of the cosmos, threads twist and bind,
Lost in the fabric, our fates intertwined.
Eons whisper our names, in love and in plea,
Our spirits entwined, forever to be.

Stars tell our story, in the night sky so clear,
Through galaxies vast, our souls draw near.
Time dances around us, a playful delight,
In eternity's grasp, we hold on tight.

Dreams echo our journey, in the quiet of space,
Two hearts lost in orbit, find their embrace.
Infinite moments, together we roam,
Entangled in eternity, we find our home.

Shadows Clasping Light

In the realm where shadows clasp the light,
The dusk and dawn share a tender sight.
Contrasts blend in a delicate dance,
In this twilight world, we find our chance.

Silhouettes whisper to the glowing moon,
Tales of the sun, that will return soon.
Midnight and morning, in sweet embrace,
In their union, time finds its grace.

The dance of darkness with beams so bright,
Creates a symphony in the night.
Where shadows clasp light, they coexist,
In their gentle hold, the world is kissed.

A balance between the night and day,
Where contrasts meet and find their way.
Shadows clasping light, in endless flight,
In their embrace, we see the world right.

The Embrace of Dawn

With gentle hands, the dawn does embrace,
The sleeping world in its tender grace.
Whispers of light, painting the sky,
A canvas of hope, in the morning high.

Birds sing in chorus, as day unfolds,
The melody of life, as it beholds.
New beginnings, in the sun's warm gaze,
In the embrace of dawn, we find our ways.

The golden hues, a promise anew,
Bathing the earth in a rosy hue.
Every dawn, an eternal vow,
To renew our hearts, and show us how.

With every sunrise, we rise again,
Shedding the shadows of yesterday's pain.
The embrace of dawn, gentle and kind,
In its light, our true path we find.

Souls Knit in Silence

In the quietude where whispers dwell,
Two souls knit in silence, a story they tell.
Without a word, their spirits speak,
A bond so strong, yet ever so meek.

Through silent stares and soft-touch hands,
In unspoken language, each understands.
The world moves on, in noise and din,
But in their silence, love does begin.

In the calmness, their hearts entwine,
A quiet love, both simple and divine.
Souls knit in silence, a rare find,
A tranquil union, uniquely designed.

In the hush of night, under the moon's glow,
Their silent love continues to grow.
Through seasons and years, they remain in tune,
Souls knit in silence, a silent boon.

Resonating Through the Reeds

In a serene and unseen glade, whispers carry far,
Between the reeds, where shadows play beneath the star.
Notes float gently, a symphony so sweet,
Nature's own orchestra, where earth and heaven meet.

A lonely flute, the wind itself, breathes life anew,
Its melody, a timeless song, amidst the dew.
Each note a story, a legacy reprieved,
Through every breath, the soul of the forest breathed.

As dusk approaches, the air with magic fills,
And in the heart of night, tranquility instills.
The melody, now a soft echo, in the reeds it hides,
Resonating endlessly, where mystery resides.

Melodies Mingled in the Mist

Far beyond where the eye can see, under the sky's gray dome,
Melodies mingled in the mist, calling the wanderer home.
The path obscured, but in the air, a song so clear,
Guiding steps, through the fog, drawing near.

Voices of the ancient woods, in whispers tell,
Of journeys taken within this ethereal swell.
Notes entwined with morning's frost, a chill embrace,
Invisible threads, binding time and space.

Each step reveals, through the thickening gray,
A melody unique, in the heart of day.
Fog lifts slowly, yet the music stays,
In the mist, memories and melodies always.

Eternal Bonds in Silent Words

In the quiet spaces, beyond what words can say,
Eternal bonds are whispered in the light of day.
Silent promises, that in the heart are sown,
A strength that in the quiet, has steadily grown.

Through the silent words, a shared understanding,
A connection that time can't erode, ever expanding.
Beneath the clamor, a serene exchange,
In the unsaid, lives a love that won't change.

Hand in hand, through life's ebb and flow,
In silence, deeper connections grow.
Through every hardship, every joy, every strife,
Silent words bond, the essence of life.

Memories Woven into the Fabric of Time

Every moment captured, a thread in the loom,
Weaves a tapestry rich, in the heart's spacious room.
With every color bright, and shades of gray,
Memories woven, in the fabric of day.

Laughter and tears, joys and fears,
Marked in the weave, through the years.
A pattern unique, with each life's chime,
Stories intertwined, in the fabric of time.

As years pass, the threads may fade,
But the memories etched, will never degrade.
In the weave, love's enduring rhyme,
Everlasting, in the fabric of time.

Threads of Endearance Weaving Through Hearts

In twilight's glow, threads begin to weave,
Twining lives together, they never leave.
Endearance holds, in the warp and weft,
Ties of the heart, in delicate cleft.

Under moon's watchful eyes, the threads dance,
In patterns of love, and sweet romance.
Through the fabric of time, they reach and bind,
Hearts together, leaving no one behind.

With each heartfelt touch, the threads grow strong,
Creating a tapestry, vast and long.
Endearment's thread, through time it soars,
Weaving through hearts, opening doors.

In quiet moments, the threads shimmer bright,
Guiding us gently through the night.
Endearing bonds, forever entwined,
In the tapestry of life, beautifully designed.

In the Garden of Nurtured Ties

In the garden where nurtured ties grow,
Roots entangle, in the earth below.
Branches reach out, in tender embrace,
In this sanctuary, a tranquil place.

Sunlight filters through the canopy's lace,
Illuminating every hidden space.
In this garden, relationships bloom,
Warding off loneliness, dispelling gloom.

Rippling laughter, like a gentle stream,
Waters the soil, in this dream.
Friendship's flowers, vibrant and wild,
In this garden, every soul's beguiled.

Seasons change, but the garden thrives,
In the soil of love, every plant revives.
In the garden of nurtured ties,
Every moment, a new bond lies.

Embracing Echoes of Shared Laughter

In the chambers of memory, echoes play,
Laughter shared, in the light of day.
Echoes bounce, in corners of the mind,
In these sounds, our spirits find.

Through years that pass, echoes grow,
In shared mirth, our connections show.
Laughter's echo, a timeless song,
In its melody, we all belong.

In every echo, there's warmth, there's light,
Bridging our hearts, through day and night.
Shared laughter, in its gentle clasp,
A bond unbroken, in its grasp.

Echoes of laughter, in the air weave,
Memories of joy, together cleave.
In the symphony of echoed delight,
Our souls embrace, ever so tight.

Whispers of the Soul's Kinship

In the silence, whispers softly rise,
Carrying secrets, under the skies.
Souls reach out, in tender kinship's call,
In these whispers, we never fall.

Beneath the cacophony of the day,
Whispers of kinship, show the way.
Gentle nudges, in the quietude,
In soulful whispers, our hearts elude.

In the softness of a whispered word,
Kinship's bonds, silently stirred.
Invisible threads, in whispers twine,
Connecting souls, in design divine.

Through whispered dreams, our spirits dance,
In the realm of kinship, we take a chance.
Whispers carry, through time and space,
In their softness, our hearts embrace.

The Lighthouse of Familiar Hearts

Above the cliffs, so stark and sheer,
A lighthouse stands, the night to peer.
Its beam cuts through the fog so white,
Guiding lost souls back to the light.

Through years and storms, it stands alone,
Its steadfast light steadily shone.
A beacon for those hearts adrift,
In seas of time, it's their gift.

Families torn by fate and chance,
In its glow, find their stance.
Waves of life may ebb and flow,
But the lighthouse keeps its constant glow.

Through windows, warm light spills,
Bridging gaps, healing ills.
In its beam, a path we find,
Back to the hearts we left behind.

Tides of Fondness Everflowing

In depths of night, under moon's soft glow,
The tides of fondness everflow.
Whispers of waves on a distant shore,
Speak of love's embrace, forevermore.

With each tide that comes and goes,
A memory in its water flows.
Kisses stolen in the dark,
Promises made in love's spark.

Seashells hold our laughter tight,
Carried far into the night.
In each grain of sand, a tale,
Of love that travels, without fail.

So let the tides come, as they will,
With fondness, our hearts they fill.
Everflowing, without end,
In love's ocean, we softly blend.

Entwined Roots of Separated Lives

Beneath the earth, where no one sees,
Lie entwined roots of towering trees.
Separated above, together below,
In secret depths, they silently grow.

Through storms and seasons, they remain,
Bound by roots, through drought and rain.
A tapestry woven underground,
Where silent whispers are the only sound.

Though branches may reach for different skies,
The roots below share silent cries.
Drawing strength from the same ancient ground,
Their lives are silently bound.

This hidden union, firm and deep,
Promises each soul to keep.
For even separated lives find,
A connection of the most enduring kind.

Beacon Fires on Lonely Nights

On hills high and mountains bold,
Beacon fires burn, stories told.
Guiding lights for those who roam,
A signal flare, calling them home.

Through the dark, a radiant light,
Pierces the veil of the night.
Lonely wanderers find their way,
By the glow of the beacon's stay.

Each flame, a hope in the dark,
A kindled spark, a mark.
In its warmth, solace we find,
Leaving shadows far behind.

So when nights grow cold and dire,
Look upon the beacon's fire.
A reminder, no matter the night's fright,
There's a warmth, a glow, an everlasting light.

Wrapped in the Glow of Tender Souls

In twilight's embrace, hearts gently unfold,
Beneath stars that whisper tales untold.
Souls entwine in the night's soft caress,
Each touch, each glance, a tender confess.

In the silence, our spirits speak loud,
Words unspoken, promises avowed.
In the glow of the moon's gentle light,
Souls dance, wrapped in the blanket of night.

Embers of love, in the quiet, they glow,
A bond that deepens, in stillness, it grows.
In the hush, our connected fates align,
Under the watchful gaze of the divine.

In the night's soft cloak, we find our release,
In the quiet, our souls find peace.
Wrapped in the glow of tender souls' embrace,
We find a love that time cannot erase.

Kindred Spirits Dancing in the Rain

With drops falling, our laughter ascends,
Barefoot on earth, where the soul mends.
Kindred spirits, in rain, we dance,
In each puddle, a reflection, a chance.

Twirling under the storm's grey skies,
In each other, our sanctuary lies.
Raindrops mingle with joyful tears,
Washing away all our fears.

Hand in hand, in the downpour, we spin,
Finding the magic that lies within.
In the rain, our true selves we reveal,
In its honesty, our spirits heal.

Dancing in the rain, our hearts speak,
Of strength found when we're feeling weak.
In this moment, no need to explain,
For love thrives, dancing in the rain.

The Melody of Mingling Breaths

In the quietude of the nearing night,
Our breaths mingle, a symphony bright.
Hearts in harmony, in silence we speak,
In every sigh, a promise we seek.

Close together, in the fading light,
Our shadows merge, becoming one sight.
Breaths interlace, a tender embrace,
In this serenade, time we outpace.

Whispers carry our dreams on the breeze,
Love's melody flows with such ease.
The rhythm of us, soft and profound,
In mingling breaths, our essences found.

In the depth of night, under star's gleam,
Together we drift, in a shared dream.
Our breaths a melody, gentle and sweet,
In their unity, our love complete.

Shared Visions in the Mirror of Time

In the mirror of time, our eyes meet,
Shared visions of paths under our feet.
Past and future in the present blend,
In our gaze, beginnings and ends mend.

Souls connected through time's flowing stream,
In our reflections, shared dreams gleam.
Through eyes that have seen a thousand years,
We recognize our joys and our fears.

In the mirror's depth, our stories unfold,
Tales of warmth, of love, and of cold.
Hand in hand, through time, we glide,
In our shared visions, we confide.

Through the glass of time, our spirits soar,
Bound by a love that is something more.
In the mirror, our destinies entwine,
Shared visions in the passage of time.

The Symphony of Linked Fates

In whispers soft, the winds convey,
A tale of souls, intertwined in fray.
Under the moon's vigilant glow,
Their destinies entwine, a seamless flow.

In the heart's deep orchestra, notes align,
A symphony of fate, both yours and mine.
Timbre of joy, and pitches of pain,
In harmony, together they remain.

Each beat, a step on paths unknown,
Guided by stars in the night sky shown.
The melody of life, complex and sweet,
In synchrony, our hearts beat.

A crescendo of dreams in the night,
Under the canopy of endless light.
Together we stand, in the vast expanse,
In the symphony of fate, we dance.

Twilight Conversations Under Shared Stars

Beneath the veil of twilight's blush,
We speak in hushed tones, in the evening's hush.
Secrets like leaves, in the wind they flutter,
Under shared stars, our hopes we utter.

The moon, a silent witness to our dreams,
Casting its glow on gentle streams.
The night air carries our whispered tales,
As we traverse life's winding trails.

In the sanctuary of night's embrace,
Our true selves we dare to face.
With every word, our spirits soar,
Finding solace in each other, evermore.

Stars twinkle above in harmonious conversation,
Mirroring the joy of our shared elation.
In the quiet of the night, under the sky so vast,
We talk of the present, the future, and the past.

Bridges Spanning Heart to Heart

Across the chasm, wide and deep,
Where thoughts swirl and emotions leap.
A bridge of words, forged strong and true,
Connects my beating heart to you.

With every step, the gap narrows,
Beneath the weight of joys and sorrows.
Hand in hand, we venture across,
Turning our losses into dross.

The mortar of trust, the bricks of care,
In each other's burdens, we learn to share.
The arc of understanding, gracefully composed,
In the language of love, our hearts disclosed.

Through storms and sunshine, the bridge does stand,
A testament to the strength of joining hand in hand.
Spanning heart to heart, across time and space,
It's a journey of love, a never-ending embrace.

Unfurling the Scrolls of Timeless Bonds

In the quiet of the night, we unfold,
The scrolls of memories, tales untold.
Each line a testament to what we've shared,
A bond so deep, nothing else compared.

Through pages of laughter, and chapters of tears,
Our story unfolds, transcending the years.
Ink of joy, and parchment of pain,
Together we've weathered, together remain.

These scrolls bear witness to the strength of our tie,
A connection so profound, it spans the sky.
In the script of our lives, our spirits entwine,
In every word, a promise divine.

As we read aloud, the past comes alive,
Each verse a step, on which we thrive.
Unfurling the scrolls, under the moon's gentle light,
Our timeless bonds gleaming ever so bright.

Echoes of Old Laughter

In halls hallowed by time's slow dance,
Where shadows play in silence's trance,
Echoes of laughter, once vivid and bright,
Now whisper soft tales in the cool moonlight.

Memories linger, in every stone crease,
Of joy once held, in the heart's release,
Each echo, a story, a moment reborn,
In the quiet dusk and the fresh of morn.

These ancient walls, now silent and still,
Once rang with laughter, a river's trill,
That flowed through the heart, with love's sweet sound,
In those echoes of old, where happiness is found.

Though the laughter has faded, its essence remains,
In the gentle breeze and the soft rain's refrains,
In the echoes of old, laughter's spirit is cast,
In the magic of memories, forever to last.

Glimpses of You in Everything

In the sunset's glow, your face I see,
In every shade of the whispering tree,
With every breeze, your laughter rings,
In my heart, your echo softly sings.

The stars at night, in their endless grace,
Hold glimpses of you, in time's embrace,
Each sparkle, a memory, a moment shared,
In the night's quiet, your presence is bared.

In the rustling leaves, your whispers I catch,
In the morning dew, your essence I snatch,
With every sunrise, in light anew,
The world awakens, filled with hues of you.

Your spirit dances, in the rain's soft cry,
In the rainbow's arc, across the sky,
In every wonder, in every sigh,
Glimpses of you, in everything, lie.

Preserved Promises

In the heart's vault, where secrets sleep,
Where echoes of promises, we silently keep,
Each word, a memento, preserved with care,
In the hush of moments, we once did share.

Like leaves encased in amber's tight grip,
Our promises linger, they never slip,
Each a beacon, in time's vast sea,
Guiding us back, to where we meant to be.

Through storms and calm, they stand resolute,
In our memories' garden, they take root,
Growing stronger, with each passing year,
Our preserved promises, forever near.

In silence, they speak, in the heart's deep well,
Of love's tender tales, they ever tell,
Preserved and cherished, in the soul's embrace,
Our promises endure, through time and space.

Immortal Flames of Bonding

In the forge of life, where hearts are tried,
In the relentless flow of time's great tide,
A bond is formed, in fire's fierce embrace,
An immortal flame, time cannot erase.

Through trials and joys, it burns ever bright,
A beacon of love, in the darkest night,
Through years and tears, it stands undimmed,
In the bond we share, love is hymned.

Not by words, but in silent strength,
It spans the heart's entire length,
A radiant blaze, in the soul's deep night,
Guiding us forth, with its unwavering light.

In every moment, with every breath,
Beyond the bounds of life and death,
Our bonds, a fire, forever flame,
In their light, we are never the same.

Harmony in the Hum of Night

Beneath the canopy of starlit grace,
Where shadows dance with light's soft embrace.
The cricket's chorus fills the void of sound,
In nature's harmony, our hearts are found.

Within the silence of the darkened sky,
The moon whispers tales as the night goes by.
Each star a note in the celestial song,
In unity, the world sings along.

The rustle of the leaves, the gentle breeze,
Together weave the symphony of peace.
As darkness holds the earth in its gentle sight,
We find a common song in the hum of night.

Nourishing the Seedlings of Sympathy

In the garden of humanity, we sow,
Kindness, the seedlings of sympathy to grow.
Watered with compassion, under the sun's glow,
In the soil of love, these tender shoots show.

With gentle hands, we tend the fragile sprouts,
Nurturing warmth that never runs out.
A kindness shared, a gentle word, a smile,
Helps these seedlings flourish, mile after mile.

In each act of care, a new leaf unfurls,
Sympathy blooms, in this world it swirls.
A garden rich with empathy's sweet scent,
The fruits of our labor, time well spent.

As the seasons change, these plants will thrive,
In the soil of understanding, they come alive.
Sympathy's roots, deep and strong, they dive,
In the heart of humanity, they will forever survive.

The Sacred Ember of Fellowship

In the heart of night, a flame burns bright,
A sacred ember, glowing with light.
It draws us near, from far and wide,
In its warmth, we find where our trust abides.

Around this fire, stories are told,
Of legends new and memories old.
A bond is forged, firm and deep,
In this fellowship, our souls leap.

Amidst the shadows, this ember's glow,
Illuminates the path we're to follow.
Hand in hand, through thick and thin,
Together, we face what lies within.

This flame of fellowship, pure and true,
Burns in our hearts, bright and new.
Through every trial, every test,
It's this sacred bond that brings out our best.

Snowflakes Merging in the Dance of Winter

In the heart of winter's embrace,
Snowflakes fall, each in its place.
Drifting down from heavens wide,
In their dance, our worlds collide.

Each flake, a masterpiece so rare,
Moves with grace, through the chilly air.
Together, they weave a tapestry white,
A blanket of peace, under the night.

In silence, they meld, each unique shape,
Creating scenes no human could drape.
Mountains, valleys, on landscapes vast,
In the dance of winter, their fates are cast.

This delicate ballet of ice and light,
Brings a magic to the longest night.
The snowflakes' dance, a silent hymn,
Uniting earth and sky at whim.

Unseen Ties That Bind

In places unseen, threads silkily twine,
Binding us gently, your essence and mine.
Through whispers of night, through beams of the day,
Invisible bonds guide us on our way.

In laughter and tears, in joy and in strife,
The ties that connect us breathe life into life.
Through seasons and years, thickest fog to clear skies,
These unseen ties hold, in silent goodbyes.

In dreams where we wander, in paths that we cross,
The fabric of us, never counting the cost.
A tapestry woven with care and with time,
In every heartbeat, your rhythm and rhyme.

In the hush of the evening, in the break of the dawn,
The unseen ties pull, ensuring we're drawn.
Back to each other, through distance and night,
Our souls intertwined, forever in flight.

Shared Silences, Sacred Words

In our shared silences, our spirits converse,
Speaking in volumes, passionate and terse.
With every pause, every breath unspoken,
We find our bond, unblemished and unbroken.

Sacred words whispered in the still of the night,
Carry our dreams, taking silent flight.
In the quiet, a sanctuary we find,
Words and silence, beautifully intertwined.

In our glances, a world of stories untold,
Shared silences, where our futures unfold.
In these moments, quiet fills the air,
Speaking sacred words, in the haven we share.

Together we stand, in the silence and the speech,
In the sacred words, our souls reach.
In shared silences, our hearts roam free,
Bonded for eternity, you and me.

Together Through Lifetimes

Through lifetimes we wander, souls entwined,
Paths crossing and merging, through time we're aligned.
In each new beginning, our spirits greet,
Together through lifetimes, our hearts beat.

In the flow of the river, the rush of the breeze,
Our connection endures, with elegant ease.
Through eras and ages, in whispers and thunder,
Our souls together, a world of wonder.

In laughter and tears, in joy and in sorrow,
Our togetherness, a beacon for tomorrow.
Through countless lifetimes, in myriad ways,
Together we shine, through the haze.

Eternal companions, through time's vast expanse,
In hand we journey, through life's intricate dance.
Together through lifetimes, a bond so true,
Eternally, delightfully, me and you.

Crescendo of Coupled Pulse

In the symphony of our intertwined beats,
Where every throb promises never to cheat.
Our hearts dance to a rhythm so intense,
In love's grasp, we lose all pretense.

With every touch, a spark ignites,
A fiery passion that the soul invites.
Two pulses in perfect harmony,
A crescendo of love, wild and free.

In your eyes, I see the universe expand,
Holding the cosmos within the palm of your hand.
Our love, a melody that soars and dives,
A testament to how truly love thrives.

Under the moon's watchful eyes, we confess,
In each other's arms, we find solace and bless.
The world fades away, leaving only you and me,
In our coupled pulse, we are truly free.

Brushstrokes on the Canvas of Togetherness

With tender strokes, we paint our days,
Colors of joy, in myriad ways.
Each hue a note in our shared song,
In the canvas of togetherness, we belong.

Your laughter, a hue of the brightest gold,
My whispers, shades of secrets untold.
Together, we blend into a masterpiece,
In our world, time seems to cease.

Through trials, our brushstrokes never fade,
In each other, our trust is deeply laid.
A tapestry of moments, rich and rare,
In the art of love, we make our share.

With each day, our canvas expands,
Embracing the future with open hands.
Our togetherness, a painting divine,
In every brushstroke, our souls intertwine.

Ode to the Intermingling of Spirits

In the realm where spirits softly merge,
Whispers of love begin to surge.
Two souls entwine in a dance so fine,
In the intermingling, their light does shine.

A touch, a glance, a shared heartbeat,
In this space, two worlds meet.
A fusion of dreams, desires, and fears,
Together, transcending the sum of our years.

Hand in hand, through storms we navigate,
In our union, destiny we orchestrate.
A tapestry woven from threads of fate,
In the melding of souls, we find our state.

Gentle is the night when together we lay,
In the merging of spirits, night turns to day.
With each breath, our love deeper grows,
The beauty of unity, forever it shows.

Cradling the Light of Common Souls

In the heart of the night, under star's gentle gaze,
Together we wander through life's intricate maze.
Cradling the light within each other's soul,
In our shared warmth, we become whole.

In laughter and tears, our spirits entwine,
In the glow of our love, eternally we shine.
Through joy and sorrow, our hearts converse,
In the symphony of life, we immerse.

Our souls, a beacon in love's sacred fire,
In each other, we find what our hearts desire.
A common flame, burning bright and true,
In the light of common souls, love finds its cue.

Together, we stand against the tides of fate,
In unity, our spirits resonate.
Hand in hand, in light and shadow's play,
Cradling the light, together we stay.

Hearts Entwined in Time

In the garden where time stands still,
We walk together, by our own will.
Our hearts beat as one, in silent rhyme,
Entwined forever, beyond the chime.

Through seasons that change, from Spring to Fall,
Our love remains steadfast, through it all.
In each other's gaze, eternity we find,
A bond so deep, it transcends time.

With every step, our souls do weave,
A tapestry of love, in which we believe.
The threads of fate, so finely spun,
Link our hearts together, two becoming one.

In this journey of life, we take our place,
With hands clasped tight, we face.
Every challenge, every climb,
Our hearts entwined, in timeless time.

Embracing Souls

Beneath the cloak of the starry night,
Two souls embrace, holding tight.
The world fades away, out of sight,
In their union, they find their light.

Whispers soft, like the breeze,
Convey love's timeless decrees.
In each other, they find their peace,
A sanctuary, where all fears cease.

Hearts pulsing with a synchronous beat,
In this embrace, they feel complete.
A connection so profound and sweet,
A love story, none can defeat.

Through trials and time, they'll always find,
A way back to each other, undefined.
Souls intertwined, in love's bind,
Embracing eternally, two of a kind.

Eternal Bonds Unbroken

Across the ages, through the sands of time,
Our spirits dance, forever entwine.
An ancient love, so pure and divine,
Creating bonds, unbroken by design.

Through tempests and trials, we stand strong,
Hand in hand, where we belong.
Our love's melody, an endless song,
In harmony, we move along.

In the echoes of the universe, our whispers soar,
Telling tales of love, folklore.
Eternal bonds, who could ask for more?
Unbroken, we explore, what life has in store.

With each sunrise, our love renews,
Bright as the day, honest and true.
Through the journey, our essence imbues,
Eternal bonds, forever anew.

Love's Everlasting Embrace

In the stillness of the night, your love wraps me tight,
A comfort against the cold, a guiding light.
In your arms, I find my place,
Lost in the warmth of love's everlasting embrace.

With every heartbeat, our love grows deep,
A promise we make, a vow we keep.
Through storms and calm, we hold on fast,
In love's embrace, we are vast.

Words unspoken, feelings unfurled,
In your eyes, I see my world.
A bond so strong, it can't be erased,
Held together, in love's everlasting embrace.

Through years and memories, we thread our story,
In moments of both sorrow and glory.
Together we stand, in time's relentless race,
Forever bound in love's everlasting embrace.

Flames of Affinity in the Hearth of Being

In the quiet core of night, where embers glow,
Softly, warmly, a subtle heart's beating.
Flames flicker, a dance of shadows and light,
A symphony of warmth, in the cold, retreating.

Beneath the canvas of our shared dreams,
Sparks of connection, in the dark, gleaming.
Gentle whispers in the crackle and pop,
Messages of hope, in the fire, streaming.

Hands clasped, eyes locked, spirits high,
The hearth of affinity, in love, believing.
Minds meld, in the glow of mutual regard,
A promise of togetherness, ever weaving.

In the flicker of flames, a future bright,
With every spark, our bond, strengthening.
Together we stand, against the night,
In the warmth of love, forever basking.

Constellations of Companionship in the Night Sky

Above, the night unfurls its jeweled tapestry,
Each star, a beacon of stories untold.
Together, they form clusters of memories,
Constellations of companionship, bold.

In the dark abyss, they shine ever bright,
Guiding wanderers, through the night.
In their light, a tale of unity is spun,
A testament to friendships, won.

With every gaze, we chart their course,
Finding solace in their heavenly force.
In the vast silence, a whispered truth,
Of enduring bonds, formed in our youth.

Through the ages, these stars have led,
In their eternal dance, our paths are wed.
The night sky, a canvas of our connection,
In its expanse, we find reflection.

Footprints Beside Mine on the Journey

Along the winding paths of fate,
Where destiny's footsteps resonate.
There beside me, a presence felt,
In the journey's fabric, seamlessly dealt.

Through valleys low and mountains high,
Beneath the vast, embracing sky.
Your footprints lay close to mine,
In life's dance, intricately entwine.

In moments of despair and glee,
Side by side, as it should be.
Sharing laughter, enduring pain,
In sunshine's warmth and in rain.

Guiding each other through unknown lands,
With gentle words and clasping hands.
The journey long, the spirits strong,
Togetherness, our most enduring song.

And when our paths seem to diverge,
A new route, together, we'll forge.
For in life's journey, come what may,
It's the footprints beside mine that guide the way.

The Whispering of Leaves in Our Shared Autumn

Seasons turn, from green to gold,
In the whispered tales, our stories told.
The rustling leaves, in the autumn wind,
A symphony of change, intimately pinned.

Each leaf a note in the melody of fall,
Singing of summers, winters, and the call.
Of springs that came and autumns that fade,
In the cycle of life, our memories laid.

Together, we watch the changing hue,
In the whispering leaves, I find you.
A shared silence, a comfort deep,
In the autumn's embrace, our promises keep.

As leaves dance in the crisp, cool air,
Our spirits lifted, a love affair.
With every season, more deeply known,
In the whispering leaves, our love has grown.

And when the last leaf falls to the ground,
In its descent, a peace is found.
For in our shared autumn, a truth rings clear,
In every whisper, I feel you near.

The Bouquet of Gathered Affections

In fields of bloom where love's seeds awake,
With tender care, each petal we partake.
A tapestry of hues, emotions blend,
In bouquets of affection that we send.

Through seasons' shift, these blossoms may wilt,
Yet, in their essence, no guilt is built.
For every moment's joy they have lent,
In memories, they remain, content.

With every dawn, new blooms shall arise,
Gathered in baskets of sweet surprise.
Affections bloom, in myriad arrays,
In the garden of hearts, love always stays.

In whispered hues, each bouquet confesses,
Tales of love, in its infinite dresses.
Through time's relentless, ever-changing mirth,
Affections gathered, adorn this earth.

Reaching Across the Expanse of Apathy

Across the vast expanse of apathy,
A bridge of compassion we try to be.
With steps unsure, in the fog of disdain,
Reaching out, to soothe the invisible pain.

In the silence where empathy grows dim,
Through acts of kindness, light edges in.
A hand extends, breaking barriers unseen,
In landscapes barren, a glint of green.

Words, like soft rain, on hardened ground fall,
Nurturing hope where despair had its thrall.
From the chasms of indifference we rise,
Building bridges, under stormy skies.

For every soul adrift, disconnected,
A beacon of understanding reflected.
Across the expanse, our spirits reach,
In every act of love, we warmly preach.

Sketching the Contours of Mutual Existence

In the canvas of time, we find a space,
Sketching contours of our shared embrace.
With strokes of experience, shades of trust,
In the gallery of life, thrive we must.

Each line a story, a memory made,
In the tapestry of kinship displayed.
Hands entwined, drawing paths yet unknown,
In mutual existence, we have grown.

Shadows of conflict, in light resolved,
In the depth of our being, deeply involved.
Chiaroscuro of love and pain,
In the art of living, we gain.

In every stroke, a harmony found,
In our shared existence, we are bound.
Through the contours of our mutual creation,
We discover the beauty of relation.

Glimpses Through the Keyhole of Kinship

Through the keyhole of kinship, glimpses see,
Of a world where hearts are bound yet free.
In the quiet rooms of understanding dwell,
Where stories of silent affections swell.

A tapestry woven from threads of care,
In the fabric of moments that we share.
Through the lens of connection deeply peered,
In the corridors of kinship, love endeared.

In whispers and glances, sentiments convey,
In the warmth of kinship, fears allay.
Through the keyhole, a vista wide and deep,
In the embrace of kinship, promises we keep.

Forging bonds in the warmth of gentle kin,
Through shared trials and triumphs, together we spin.
In glimpses through kinship, together we rhyme,
In the dance of existence, through time.

Grasping Hands Through the Mist of Years

In the quiet haze of passing time,
Where echoes dance and intertwine,
We reach through years, a ceaseless quest,
Grasping hands, in hope, we jest.

Amidst the mist, our fingers brush,
Tales of old, in whispers hush,
Memories faint, yet feelings keen,
In the distance, barely seen.

Through veils of time, our spirits seek,
A bond unspoken, strong yet meek,
Hands entangled through the haze,
Guiding each other through the maze.

In the fabric of the years spun tight,
Our hands clasp firm, holding on with might,
Through the mist, a path we carve,
In every moment, love we starve.

Time may fade, yet here we stand,
Grasping hands 'neath time's vast sand,
Together yet apart, in silent cheers,
United through the mist of years.

Dancing Shadows of Intertwined Spirits

Under the moon's gentle gleam,
Shadows dance, a silent scream,
Two spirits blend, in night's embrace,
Lost in time, a hidden space.

With every twist, a story told,
Of love and loss, of brave and bold,
Intertwined, they move as one,
Under stars, until the sun.

Their steps whisper in the dark,
A tender touch, a fleeting spark,
Shadows merge, an ethereal sight,
Dancing through the veil of night.

In every movement, love's sweet song,
Together where they truly belong,
In darkness, they find their light,
Spirits intertwined, taking flight.

As dawn breaks, shadows fade away,
But in the night, their love will stay,
Dancing spirits, forever entwined,
In shadows, their sanctuary they find.

Echoes of Intimacy in the Whispering Wind

In the soft sigh of the evening breeze,
Whispers carry with such ease,
Echoes of intimacy, delicate and grand,
Woven through the wind, across the land.

Each gust a caress, unseen yet felt,
In every silence, hearts do melt,
Wind carries tales of love's embrace,
Kisses blown, across time and space.

In every howl, in every moan,
The wind makes lovers' secrets known,
A symphony of souls, mixed in the air,
Intimacy's echo, found everywhere.

Whispers in the trees, rustling leaves attest,
To love's soft whisper, in the wind's quest,
Carrying warmth, through cold and frost,
In the whispering wind, no love is lost.

As the wind dances, so do hearts entwine,
Echoes of intimacy, forever to shine,
In every breeze, love's message sent,
Through whispering winds, hearts' content.

Blossoms of Affection in Frostbitten Grounds

In the grip of winter's chill,
Where silence roams, and time stands still,
Against all odds, a blossom grows,
Affection's warmth amidst the snows.

Through frozen soil, it reaches high,
A testament of love, beneath the icy sky,
Fragile petals, strength untold,
In frostbitten grounds, affection bold.

Each bloom a whisper, a soft caress,
In the coldest hour, love confess,
A promise made, under winter's frown,
In barren fields, love's seed sown down.

With every petal, resilience shown,
Amidst the cold, warmth is known,
Blossoms of affection, in defiance stand,
A testament to love, in frostbitten land.

As seasons turn, and warmth returns,
Love's blossoms grow, as heart yearns,
In frostbitten grounds, they bloom anew,
Affection's testament, forever true.

Melded Shadows in the Midnight Hour

In velvet cloaks, the night whispers soft,
Veiling lovers in a cradle aloft.
Melded shadows, under moon's gentle power,
Blend as one in the midnight hour.

Whispers carry through the darkened trees,
Secrets shared with the gentle breeze.
Stars blink above, a celestial shower,
Guiding dreams in their ivory tower.

Entwined fingers, a silent vow,
Pledging love in the quiet now.
Souls dancing, time seems to devour,
In the embrace of the midnight hour.

Shadows merge, a mystical art,
Painting passion straight from the heart.
Invisible threads that sweetly empower,
Lovers becoming the night's own flower.

Boundless, the moonlit path they tread,
Under the cloak where night has led.
In each other, their spirits tower,
Melded shadows in the midnight hour.

The Unseen Threads of Mutual Being

Invisible strings tie us, unseen but felt,
A tapestry of lives intricately dealt.
Each thread vibrates, a silent calling,
In the tapestry where light is falling.

Through the weave, our spirits reach,
A language of love, beyond speech.
Mutual being, a bond unbreaking,
In each other, our souls awaking.

The threads that bind us, soft and strong,
Sing the chorus of the human song.
Invisible yet as real as the morning,
Uniting souls without a warning.

These threads weave through joy and sorrow,
Promising hope for each tomorrow.
Invisible hands, life's loom entwining,
With every twist, our destinies aligning.

Unseen but felt, this fabric of life,
Cuts through darkness, like a knife.
In mutual being, our hearts are threading,
Along the paths our spirits are treading.

Radiance Reflected in Each Other's Eyes

In the gaze where two souls meet,
Lies a universe where hearts beat.
A radiance born from the depths of skies,
Is the light reflected in each other's eyes.

Moments shared, a silent pact,
In looks where hidden truths are unpacked.
Through windows of soul, the world defies,
Finding home in each other's eyes.

Whispers of love in glances shared,
In the embrace of a soul bared.
Each glance, a spark that never dies,
Eternal flames in each other's eyes.

In the mirror of sight, emotions dance,
Leading hearts into a trance.
In every look, love multiplies,
Amplified in each other's eyes.

With each gaze, souls become entwined,
In the depth of eyes, true selves are defined.
Reflections of love, the highest prize,
Is radiance found in each other's eyes.

Mosaic of Moments Pieced Together

Life, a canvas, moments a hue,
Together, a picture earnest and true.
Each second a piece, a part of the tether,
In our hands, a mosaic pieced together.

Laughter and tears, the spectrum wide,
Memories within, where secrets hide.
Bright and dark, in all kinds of weather,
Bits of us, in the mosaic together.

Fragments of joy, shards of pain,
In the puzzle of life, nothing in vain.
Each fragment a treasure to gather,
In the art of moments, pieced together.

The touch of a hand, the warmth of a smile,
Are pieces that make the struggles worthwhile.
With love as the glue, we face the heather,
Creating a mosaic to cherish forever.

So we collect, from the journey we tread,
Moments like stars over our head.
Bound by time, an invisible tether,
A beautiful mosaic of moments pieced together.

Stepping Stones Over the Stream of Separation

Across the breadth of whispering streams,
Our hearts locked in an unseen seam.
Each stone a step, a hope, a dream,
Bridging gaps where light gleams.

In silence, our souls converse,
Through the void, our whispers disperse.
Each leap, a verse in our universe,
Defying the spell of the timeless curse.

Hand to hand, in spectral clasp,
We meet in memories' tender grasp.
Each stone a story, a moment to gasp,
The stream of separation in our grasp.

Between us flows the river of time,
Yet our spirits dance, intertwine.
Stepping stones of faith, sublime,
In our hearts, we cross the prime.

The Warmth of Enclosed Palms

In the heart of winter's chill,
Two palms unite, a warmth to fill.
Enclosed they stay, against the bitter draft,
A fortress of warmth, within they craft.

Through storms and frost, they remain enclosed,
A testament of warmth, opposingly posed.
In each other's grip, the cold they defy,
The warmth of unity, under the icy sky.

Moments shared, in the hearth of hands,
Where whispered secrets form silent bands.
Fingers entwined, a silent promise kept,
In the warmth of enclosed palms, tears wept.

The comfort found in another's hold,
A tale of warmth, through ages retold.
In the clasp of hands, a sanctuary found,
Where love and warmth unboundedly abound.

Dewdrops of Reminiscence on the Web of Life

Each morning brings the light, anew,
Dewdrops glisten, on threads so true.
The web of life, intricate, wide,
Holds memories like dewdrops, side by side.

In each tiny bead, a reflection found,
Of moments past, in time unbound.
A shimmering echo of laughter and tears,
Dewdrops of reminiscence, through the years.

They cling to the threads, with delicate grace,
Gleaming at dawn, in time's embrace.
Witnesses to the cycles, of moon and sun,
The web of life, where all is one.

With the warmth of day, they fade away,
But in memories, forever, they sway.
Dewdrops of the past, in the morning light,
On the web of life, a beautiful sight.

Sunsets Shared from Distant Shores

From different shores, our eyes behold,
The canvas of the sky, in hues bold.
Separated by miles, together in sight,
We share the sunset, in its fleeting light.

Orange and crimson, in harmony blend,
A moment of beauty, as day meets its end.
Each sunset, a letter, across seas sent,
In colors, our whispers of longing are vent.

Though oceans apart, in soul, we stand near,
Watching the sun dip, in reverence, here.
The horizon unites us, in its fiery embrace,
In the beauty of dusk, our hearts find grace.

As stars take their places, in the night's dome,
We find solace, knowing we're never alone.
Sunsets shared, from distant lands,
Connect our hearts, as night expands.

Quiet Moments of Unspoken Understandings

In the silence between us, a language blooms,
Soft glances carry messages, filling all the rooms.
Words unneeded, for our hearts converse,
In quiet moments, our souls immerse.

Underneath the cacophony of the day,
Whispers of comprehension in the air sway.
Eyes meet, and in them, stories are told,
Of understanding deep, neither bought nor sold.

Hands brush, a silent promise made,
In the sanctuary of silence, all doubts fade.
Between heartbeats, a connection so profound,
In unspoken understandings, we are bound.

In the quietude, our spirits dance,
Invisible threads of trust enhance.
No words uttered, yet everything known,
In quiet moments, our understanding has grown.

In the stillness, our souls speak louder than words,
A symphony of silence, in unseen chords.
In these moments, so quietly bright,
We find strength in our silent, shared light.

Ripples in the Pond of Togetherness

Together, we cast stones in life's vast pond,
Watching ripples form, to the beyond.
Each wave, a memory, a shared delight,
In the pond of togetherness, shimmering bright.

Our laughs, the pebbles that disturb the calm,
Creating waves of joy, a soothing balm.
Moments ripple out, touching distant shores,
In this water, our togetherness soars.

With every ripple, our bond strengthens, grows,
Through ebbs and flows, our communal heart knows.
Together, creating patterns so divine,
In the tapestry of time, beautifully we entwine.

Ripples merging, in the dance of fate,
Our togetherness, a state we cultivate.
In the pond of life, our reflections seen,
Together, we navigate the spaces between.

Hand in hand, we face each day anew,
Creating ripples of a love so true.
In the pond of togetherness, we find,
A sanctuary for the heart and mind.

The Quilt of Comforting Presences

In the fabric of our days, threads intertwine,
Creating a quilt of comfort, design divine.
Each stitch, a moment of shared laughter or tear,
In the warmth of this quilt, we harbor no fear.

Patchwork of memories, each square unique,
Stories of comfort, in the threads that speak.
Together, under this blanket, we find repose,
In the quilt of presence, our shared love glows.

Threads woven from the heart, with care,
In each fiber, a promise to always be there.
Colors blend, in the warmth of affection's embrace,
In this quilt, every worry we face.

Through the cold, through the nights long and deep,
This quilt of comforting presences, we keep.
A reminder of love, in every seam,
In this quilt, we dream our collective dream.

Wrapped in layers of gentle, holding tight,
In our quilt, every sorrow takes flight.
In the comfort of presences, together we rest,
In this quilt, we are forever blessed.

Silhouettes of Closeness on Horizon's Edge

On the edge of horizon, where dreams are born,
Our silhouettes merge, in the breaking dawn.
Closeness that speaks, in silences vast,
In the moment fleeting, a future cast.

Shadows intertwine, under the moon's soft glow,
In the dance of night, our companionship grows.
Outlined against the sky, two forms as one,
In the silhouette of closeness, never undone.

As the sun dips low, painting skies in hue,
Our merged outlines, in the twilight brew.
In this closeness, no words need to be said,
In our silhouette, our stories thread.

The horizon stretches, endless and wide,
Yet, in our closeness, no need to hide.
Silhouettes against the world, stark and clear,
In our unity, we have nothing to fear.

With the dawning light, a new day embraced,
Our silhouettes of closeness, never erased.
On the horizon's edge, a testament so true,
In our silhouette, our bond renews.

Infinite Threads of Joy

Beneath a canvas of endless blue,
We trace the threads of joy anew.
A tapestry rich, with bright hue interlaced,
Where moments of bliss are forever chased.

With every dawn, the sun's golden rays,
Weave into our hearts, in mysterious ways.
Each thread shimmering in morning's light,
Binding us in warmth, banishing the night.

Laughter echoes, in spaces vast and wide,
Creating ripples, where happiness abides.
Infinite threads, in colors unseen,
Sew together dreams, both remembered and been.

In the heart of night, under starlit skies,
Our woven joy, quietly lies.
It breathes in whispers, soft and low,
In every stitch, our affection grows.

A fabric made, from love's own hands,
Spans across time, in countless strands.
Infinite threads of joy, forever entwined,
In the fabric of life, beautifully defined.

Holding Echoes in our Hands

In the silence of the past, echoes call,
Holding moments fragile, lest they fall.
We grasp them tight, with gentle care,
Fearing the void, should they disappear.

Whispers of yesteryears, in our grasp,
A collection of memories, we clasp.
Each echo, a story, a frozen scene,
Preserved in the mind, forever keen.

Through the corridors of time, we stroll,
Holding echoes in our hands, a toll.
For every laugh, every tear we've shed,
Becomes a part of the path we tread.

In the palms of our hands, they lay,
Soft echoes of the past, in display.
A poignant reminder of what has been,
In the echoes we hold, life's seen.

These echoes, a treasure, a gift so rare,
In the quiet, with us, they share.
A bond with the past, unbreakably strong,
In our hands, where all echoes belong.

Heartbeats Synced in Silence

In the quietude of the unspoken night,
Our heartbeats synch, in the muted light.
No words pass between, no sound to be heard,
Just the silent agreement, without a word.

Beneath the canopy of a star-studded sky,
The rhythm of our pulses, a soft lullaby.
In the silence, our hearts communicate,
A language of love, that we silently state.

In each other's gaze, a conversation deep,
A pact we made, in silence, to keep.
Heartbeats in harmony, in the quiet, align,
In the silent spaces, where souls intertwine.

With every touch, every glance exchanged,
Our silent pact, ever unchained.
United in the quiet, our hearts find their pace,
In the hush of the night, a sacred space.

So, in the silence, let our heartbeats sing,
A melody of love, in silent spring.
Synced in the quiet, a bond so deep,
In the silence, our promises, we keep.

Silent Pact Beyond Words

In the spaces between words, our pact was made,
A silent agreement, in the shade.
No vows spoken, no promises said,
Yet in our hearts, the pledge was laid.

Through glances, a language only we understand,
In the silent moments, hand in hand.
A connection profound, beyond verbal art,
A silent pact, from heart to heart.

In the quiet, our spirits intertwine,
A bond unseen, yet clear, defined.
Through every breath, and every sigh,
Our silent pact, under the open sky.

No need for words, when souls connect,
A silent vow, we silently protect.
Through the rhythms of life, together we dance,
In the realm of silence, a deep romance.

So let the world speak, in noise, in fray,
Our silent pact, leads the way.
In the hush of the dawn, in the whisper of night,
Our promise endures, in the absence of light.

The Quiet Strength of Us

In whispers soft, beneath the moon's gentle gaze,
We find our hearts entwined, a labyrinthine maze.
Silent strength in clasped hands, a story unsung,
In the quiet of our eyes, our love is young.

Against the whirl of the world, in its fervent rush,
Our souls speak in hushes, in the twilight's blush.
In the solace of shadows, under starlit skies,
Lies the quiet strength of us, where true peace lies.

Through storms that rage, and winds that howl so fierce,
Our bond, unbreakable, their armors cannot pierce.
With whispers soft, we conquer fears, side by side,
In the quiet strength of us, we confide.

Through seasons change, and years gently fold,
Our quiet strength, a tale silently told.
In each other, we find our most courageous self,
In the quiet strength of us, our greatest wealth.

And when the final curtain falls, our journey ends,
The quiet strength of us, on which love depends.
Through whispered memories, our spirits dance,
In the quiet strength of us, love's last chance.

Faces in the Stars

With night's velvet cloak draped across the sky,
We gaze upwards, where our hopes and dreams lie.
Faces in the stars, watching over us so far,
Guiding our paths, like an ancient avatar.

In each twinkling light, a story told,
Of heroes brave, and adventurers bold.
Faces in the stars, with tales so vast,
Whispers of the future, echoes of the past.

Through the tapestry of night, their gaze meets ours,
Connecting us to distant, celestial towers.
Faces in the stars, in silence, they converse,
In their quiet commune, the universe.

Our lives, fleeting, a moment's breath,
Under the stars, we ponder life and death.
Faces in the stars, in their eternal watch,
Remind us of our journey, the onward march.

So let us live, with hearts wide open,
Under the stars, unbroken, unspoken.
Faces in the stars, in their light, we trust,
Guiding us through the darkness, as they must.

Laughter Lingering in the Air

In the glimmer of twilight, laughter finds its way,
Bounding through the fields, where children play.
A sound so sweet, it calls the heart to join,
In the symphony of joy, our spirits anoint.

Through the echoing halls, and down the bustling streets,
Laughter dances on the breeze, a melody so sweet.
It weaves through the chatter, a vibrant thread,
In the fabric of memories, it's warmly spread.

Under the canopy of stars, by the flickering firelight,
Laughter rings out, piercing the quiet night.
Stories told with chuckles, and tales with grins,
In laughter, the warmth of companionship begins.

In moments of sorrow, when tears cloud our sight,
Laughter comes like sunshine, making burdens light.
A reminder that joy, though it may hide, will return,
In laughter, our hearts once more brightly burn.

So let us cherish the laughter, lingering in the air,
An unseen bond, a comfort in despair.
For in laughter, we find strength to face the day,
In every chuckle, a beacon leading the way.

Footsteps Merged in Sand

On a beach where time seems to stand still,
Our footsteps merge in sand, a testament of will.
Side by side, we wander, lost in thought,
Leaving behind traces, of battles fought.

The horizon stretches, endless, beyond our gaze,
Echoing our dreams, in the sunlight's blaze.
Footsteps merged in sand, a journey shared,
A path unwritten, forged as we dared.

With each wave that washes ashore, our marks erased,
Reminding us that moments are fleeting, not to be chased.
Yet, in our hearts, the memories remain,
Footsteps merged in sand, amidst the sun and rain.

As the day fades, and the stars begin to gleam,
Our footsteps merged in sand, like a shared dream.
Hand in hand, we acknowledge our transient stay,
In the dance of life, where love leads the way.

So let us walk on, leaving footprints, side by side,
In the sands of time, with the tide as our guide.
For though the waves may erase what we leave behind,
In each other, our footsteps forever entwined.

Unfading Echoes of Us

In the whisper of the wind, our stories blend,
Two souls in harmony, paths that wend.
Echoes of laughter, under the sun's caress,
Shared moments, our hearts confess.

Through the corridors of time, unfading,
Our memories, like stars, ever parading.
Gentle words, soft and tender, a soothing balm,
In the silence of the night, a solace and calm.

In every sigh of the earth, in every rustling leaf,
Lies the eternal echo of our belief.
That love, once kindled in the heart's deep core,
Shall resonate forevermore.

A Canopy of Shared Dreams

Beneath a sky where dreams intertwine,
Lies a world where your heart meets mine.
A canopy of wishes, whispered at night,
Under the blanket of stars, oh so bright.

Hands clasped tightly, in hopes we believe,
Painting futures together, moments we weave.
In the fabric of dreams, our desires are sown,
On this journey of life, not alone, but grown.

With every dawn, our aspirations take flight,
In the warmth of the sun or the moon's soft light.
The promise of tomorrow, a shared dream's embrace,
Guiding us onward, together we face.

Woven in the Tapestry of Time

In the loom of the ages, our tales entwine,
Woven threads of destiny, in design divine.
Moments captured in the weave, stained with grace,
The artistry of life, time cannot erase.

Ephemeral whispers of the past, present, and future,
Intricately stitched, a seamless suture.
Memories, a myriad of hues, vivid and vibrant,
Crafting a tapestry, in every instant, significant.

From the dawn of existence, to the end of days,
Our stories interlace, in myriad ways.
Bound by the threads of fate, tightly sewn,
In the tapestry of time, our legacies are grown.

Entwined by Moonlit Memories

In the silvery glow of the moon's embrace,
Our shadows dance, together interlace.
Whispers of love, carried on the night breeze,
Moments etched in memory, designed to please.

The melody of crickets, a symphony sweet,
As moonlit memories in our hearts repeat.
Laughter and joy, under the celestial dome,
In the quiet of the night, we find our home.

With each beam that lights the darkened sky,
Our souls entwined, on dreams we fly.
Carrying hopes on the wings of the serene,
In the realm of the night, together we're seen.

Bridge Built from Heartstrings

In valleys of silence, beneath the sky's vast expanse,
Where whispers of lovers in twilight dance,
There's a bridge, not of stone, but of heartstrings and chance,
Connecting two souls in perpetual trance.

Through years it withstands, in storms and in calm,
Its foundation much deeper than any written psalm,
With each step, a melody, like a healing balm,
In a world often cold, it's a comforting warm.

Not visible to eyes, but clear to the heart,
This bridge, a masterpiece, a true work of art,
Built not by hands, but by love's silent chart,
Guiding two lives so they never part.

Across it, words travel, sentiments convey,
Bearing hopes and dreams, night and day,
In laughter and tears, in all we dare say,
The bridge stands resilient, come what may.

From heartstring to heartstring, it's carefully twined,
A testament to love, uniquely designed,
Across time and space, it's our love defined,
This bridge we traverse, with destinies aligned.

Engraved in the Essence

Upon the canvas of the universe, wide and vast,
Each star a story, each galaxy a past,
Yet, in the essence of all we amass,
Lies the engraving of moments that last.

With every sunrise, a promise anew,
In every sunset, a whisper of the view,
Life, a collection of the old and the new,
Pain and joy, etched deep and true.

In the heart's quiet corners, hidden from sight,
Are the etchings of love, glowing with light,
Memories and moments, in the day and the night,
Keeping the essence of being, ever so bright.

Like the wind carves canyons, invisible but sure,
Time engraves upon us, its lessons pure,
Each experience, a stroke, each moment a cure,
Engraved in our essence, forever to endure.

Through the journey of life, in all its resonance,
We carry within us, this innate essence,
With each breath, each step, in its magnificence,
Our souls a gallery, of living presence.

The Alchemy of Us

In the crucible of time, our lives intertwine,
A mixture so complex, so divine,
The alchemy of us, a rare design,
Transforming base metal to gold, pure and fine.

From the very first glance, a spark was lit,
In the warmth of your smile, I found my wit,
Together, a fire, neither could admit,
In the alchemy of us, perfectly fit.

With every word, a spell was cast,
In every silence, a bond so vast,
The magic of moments, built to last,
In the alchemy of us, unbreakably fast.

Through trials and tribulations, our love was tested,
In the heat of it all, beautifully bested,
Into stronger bonds, our souls were nested,
In the alchemy of us, eternally vested.

So here's to the potion, of you and I,
A concoction of love, under the infinite sky,
In the alchemist's lab, where our hearts lie,
The alchemy of us, never to say goodbye.

Beyond the Veil of Seasons

Beyond the veil of seasons, under the cloak of time,
Where days merge into years, in an endless chime,
There lies a realm, in its prime,
Where love and beauty, forever rhyme.

As spring whispers to the budding flowers,
Summer's embrace feels like gentle showers,
Autumn's colors bring the power,
And winter's chill, a silent hour.

Each season, a chapter in the earth's own tale,
A cycle of life, in which we all sail,
Yet, love remains, ever so frail,
Beyond the veil of seasons, it does prevail.

In this journey through warmth and cold,
Where stories of love and loss are told,
Our hearts, brave and bold,
Find love's true mold, in the old.

So, let us walk, hand in hand,
Beyond the veil where time is sand,
In love's ethereal land,
Where seasons bow to love's command.

Sailing the Seas of Symbiotic Souls

Across the vast, cerulean expanse,
We sail under the banner of chance,
Two souls intertwined in a rhythmic dance,
Their spirits alight, in unity, they prance.

With every wave, a new dream is spun,
Together facing the glaring sun,
Beneath the stars, their hearts beat as one,
In this journey, a new life has begun.

Sailing through storms, their bond does not fray,
In symbiotic silence, they find their way,
Whispering winds guide them, come what may,
Together, in harmony, their spirits sway.

Through uncharted waters, they dauntlessly roam,
In the vast seas, they have found a home,
No longer adrift, no longer alone,
Entwined souls, across the oceans, they comb.

Murmured Promises Under the Crescent Moon

Under the crescent moon's soft, silvery light,
Two lovers whisper, the night alight,
Promises murmured, holding each other tight,
In the cool air, their bond takes flight.

The world asleep, they share their dreams,
By the gentle glow of lunar beams,
In their eyes, a sparkling gleam,
A moment frozen, or so it seems.

Secrets shared under the starlit sky,
In each other's arms, they softly lie,
Time stands still as moments sigh,
Under the moon's watchful eye.

Promises woven into the night's embrace,
In the quiet, their hearts race,
Together in time, in this sacred space,
The night bears witness to their grace.

Bound by whispers in the night,
In each other, they find their light,
Under the crescent moon, so bright,
The dawn finds them, holding on tight.

The Alchemy of Merging Hearts

In the crucible of love, hearts meld and merge,
An alchemy divine, as emotions surge,
From two separate lives, a single song does emerge,
Through trials and time, their spirits purge.

Like molten gold, in the fire, they are remade,
In the flames, their fears and doubts fade,
Together they stand, in light and in shade,
A bond unbreakable, in the heat, it was made.

Through the alchemist's fire, their love does refine,
In each other, their souls perfectly align,
A tale as old as time, a design divine,
Within their hearts, an eternal sign.

Merging into one, their spirits soar,
In love's great furnace, they are reborn,
Together facing whatever is in store,
In each other, their true selves are sworn.

From the alchemy of hearts, a new world is wrought,
In the dance of destiny, they are caught,
Together, by fire and passion taught,
In the merging of their hearts, they find what they sought.

Mirrored in the Lakes of Each Other's Minds

In the depths of your eyes, I find my reflection,
A mirror to my soul, in your affection,
In the lakes of our minds, a silent connection,
Beyond the realms of time, in perfect projection.

Your thoughts whisper to me in quiet repose,
In your mind's lake, my own reflection grows,
Together, in our depths, a shared story flows,
In the mirrored waters, our true essence shows.

Diving deep into each other's psyche,
In your eyes, the universe I see,
A twin soul, in you, I find the key,
Mirrored minds, in each other, we are free.

In the calm waters of your soul, I dive,
In your depths, I truly feel alive,
Our minds in harmony, in love, we thrive,
In each other, our spirits arrive.

Mirrored in thought, in soul, in mind,
In each other, our true selves we find,
A connection so deep, so uniquely kind,
In the lakes of our minds, forever entwined.

Letters Written in the Wind

Words whispered, soft as a sigh,
Carried away, under the azure sky.
Invisible ink, nature's own blend,
Messages of love, the wind does send.

Paths unseen, where secrets twine,
Across distances, your heart meets mine.
Each gust a courier, wild and free,
Bearing tales across the sea.

In the hush of night, in daylight's gleam,
The wind carries our shared dream.
Through rustling leaves, over waves' crest,
Our thoughts together, find their rest.

Boundless skies, unending space,
Yet in the wind, our words embrace.
A dance of joy, sorrow, and mirth,
Letters written in the wind, finding their worth.

The Language of Glances

Eyes meet in silence, stories untold,
In their depths, a myriad of emotions unfold.
A language of glances, no words need to speak,
Tales of love, of longing, in a glimpse, a peek.

A flutter of lashes, a gaze that lingers,
Conversations held in the touch of fingers.
Within silent glances, entire worlds reside,
Secrets and promises, in the open hide.

Moments captured in the eye's embrace,
A tender look, a fiery trace.
In every glance, love's nuances dance,
A silent symphony, a captivating trance.

Eyes, the windows to the soul's vast expanse,
In each look, a chance for romance.
Through the language of glances, hearts entwine,
A dialogue divine, without a line.

Reflections of Resonance

In the mirror of the world, our souls reflect,
Echoing each other, in ways we least expect.
A resonance of life, in every shared glance,
In our mirrored paths, we find our dance.

Through the ripples of existence, our spirits call,
In the reflections, we see the rise and fall.
Our echoes meet, in the midst of time's flow,
In the water's face, our shared stories glow.

In every shadow, in every light's embrace,
Our lives intertwine, in the silent space.
Reflections of resonance, in the night's deep,
In the day's warmth, our promises keep.

Mirrored moments, in the depths we dive,
Finding in each other, reasons to thrive.
In the echoes of our beings, we understand,
Reflections of resonance, hand in hand.

Beneath the Same Sky

Under the canopy of the endless blue,
We dream our dreams, both old and new.
Beneath the same sky, our hopes take flight,
In the blanket of stars, in the moon's soft light.

Different paths we walk, yet we share the same view,
The same sun sets for me, as it does for you.
Under the same heavens, our stories unfold,
In the warmth of the sun, in the moon's cold.

Beneath the expanse of the azure dome,
We find in the sky, a shared home.
In the light of day, in the night's embrace,
We're united under the sky's vast space.

Though miles apart, under the sky we lie,
Bound by the beauty of the same high.
Beneath the same stars, our dreams we cast,
Together in spirit, in the vast.

Threads of Destiny

In the loom of time, our stories intertwine,
Beneath the skies, where dreams are confined.
With every thread, fate weaves unseen,
Connecting souls, in realms between.

Guided by stars, our paths cross and part,
A tapestry of lives, a work of art.
Destiny's hands, gentle yet firm,
Crafting the journey, at every turn.

Invisible threads, pull us close, set us free,
Tangled in the dance, of what's meant to be.
Through trials and joy, our spirits soar,
Destiny's threads, guide us to the shore.

Bound by the weave, of fate's grand design,
Our paths entwined, by threads divine.
In the fabric of time, our stories are told,
Through threads of destiny, our futures unfold.

Memories Cradled in Love

In the quiet of night, memories take flight,
Cradled in love, shining so bright.
Each tender moment, held so dear,
In the heart's cradle, love draws near.

Through the years, these memories bloom,
In the gardens of heart, there's always room.
Gentle whispers of the past, so soft, so sweet,
In the cradle of love, our hearts beat.

With every heartbeat, love's story is told,
Memories cradled, more precious than gold.
These treasures of heart, so fragile, so true,
In love's embrace, forever anew.

Hand in hand, through life we stroll,
Memories cradled, in love's gentle hold.
In the twilight of years, as we look above,
Our lives are a tapestry, woven with love.

Whispers of the Heart

In the still of night, whispers take flight,
Soft and gentle, in the moon's pale light.
Secrets of the heart, tender and true,
Carried on the breeze, just to you.

With every heartbeat, whispers grow,
Filling the silence, in their gentle glow.
Words unspoken, feelings so deep,
In the heart's sanctuary, these whispers we keep.

Through the hustle of life, they find a way,
Guiding our steps, day by day.
In every whisper, love is heard,
In every silence, hearts are stirred.

Echoes of whispers, throughout the night,
Hold us close, in their soft light.
In the heart's quiet, where whispers dwell,
The language of love, they softly tell.

A Symphony of Spirits

In the realm of twilight, where spirits soar,
A symphony plays, forevermore.
Each note a whisper, from the beyond,
In the symphony of spirits, we find our bond.

Harmony and discord, in balance they sway,
Telling stories, of night and day.
In every chord, a memory unfolds,
A symphony of spirits, in us it holds.

With each crescendo, we feel the pulse,
Of the universe's heart, in us convulse.
In the quiet moments, the softest hum,
A reminder that from the stars, we come.

Together in spirit, together in song,
In the symphony of spirits, we belong.
Through the music, our souls take flight,
In the dance of dawn, and the calm of night.

www.ingramcontent.com/pod-product-compliance
Lightning Source LLC
LaVergne TN
LVHW020422070526
838199LV00003B/235